FAST Lane
DRAG RACING

FUNNY CAR
DRAGSTERS

By Tyrone Georgiou

Gareth Stevens
Publishing

Lakewood Memorial Library
12 W. Summit Street
Lakewood, NY 14750

WITHDRAWN

DRAG RACING

Please visit our Web site, www.garethstevens.com. For a free color catalog of all our high-quality books, call toll free 1-800-542-2595 or fax 1-877-542-2596.

Library of Congress Cataloging-in-Publication Data

Georgiou, Tyrone.
 Funny car dragsters / Tyrone Georgiou.
   p. cm. — (Fast lane: Drag racing)
 Includes index.
 ISBN 978-1-4339-4696-7 (pbk.)
 ISBN 978-1-4339-4697-4 (6-pack)
 ISBN 978-1-4339-4695-0 (library binding)
 1. Drag racing—Juvenile literature. 2. Funny cars—Juvenile literature. I. Title.
 GV1029.3.G48 2011
  796.72—dc22
                                          2010025706

First Edition

Published in 2011 by
Gareth Stevens Publishing
111 East 14th Street, Suite 349
New York, NY 10003

Copyright © 2011 Gareth Stevens Publishing

Designer: Daniel Hosek
Editor: Greg Roza

Photo credits: Cover, pp. 1, 9, 11, 13 (inset), 21 Rusty Jarrett/Getty Images; p. 5 Ralph Crane/Time & Life Pictures/Getty Images; p. 7 (main image) Jonathan Ferrey/Getty Images; p. 7 (inset) Ken Levine/Getty Images; pp. 15, 17 (main image), 19 Brian Bahr/Getty Images; pp. 12–13 Shutterstock.com; p. 17 (inset) Todd Warshaw/Getty Images.

All rights reserved. No part of this book may be reproduced in any form without permission in writing from the publisher, except by a reviewer.

Printed in the United States of America

CPSIA compliance information: Batch #CW11GS: For further information contact Gareth Stevens, New York, New York at 1-800-542-2595.

CONTENTS

Words in the glossary appear in **bold** type the first time they are used in the text.

Drag racing is a contest between two motor **vehicles**. The two vehicles race side-by-side on a straight track, which is usually ¼ mile (400 m) long. The driver who reaches the finish line first is the winner!

Drag racing became an official sport in the early 1950s in California. People took their **"hot rods"** to the Mohave Desert to race. Later, they raced on airport runways in Southern California. Today, there are many kinds of drag racing. One of these is Funny Cars.

Fast Fact

A vehicle's ability is measured in top speed (mph or kph) and elapsed time (ET), or the amount of time it takes to get from the starting line to the finish line.

Thousands of fans watch a drag race in 1957.

WHAT'S A FUNNY CAR?

A Funny Car is a wild-looking car that's a little like an everyday car. The first Funny Cars took shape in the 1960s when racers started changing regular cars to make them faster. They added larger engines, bigger back tires, and smaller front tires. They also made crazy changes to the bodies.

In 1965, "Dandy" Dick Landry raced cars with so many wild changes that people said they looked "funny." The name stuck. These were the first "Funny Cars."

Fast Fact In 1982, Southern California racer Don "The Snake" Prudhomme became the first driver to go 250 miles (402 km) per hour in a Funny Car. He's also a four-time Funny Car Champion.

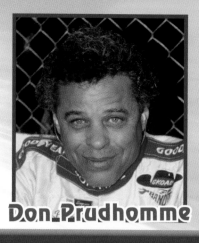

Don Prudhomme

Today's Funny Cars are specially built race cars.

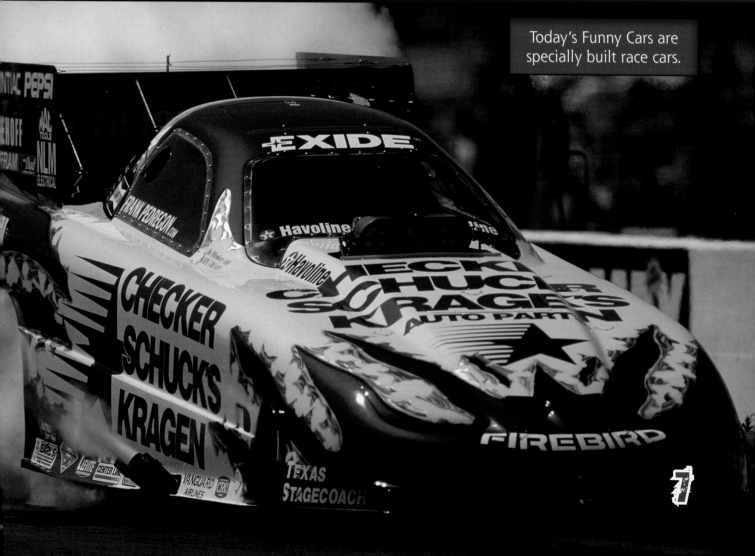

Funny Cars have large, powerful engines. A blower forces more **fuel** into the engine for extra power. A car's power is measured in horsepower (HP). An everyday car makes about 150 HP. A Funny Car makes 8,000 HP! This destroys the engine, and it must be completely rebuilt after every race.

Funny Cars use a special powerful fuel called nitromethane. Because of this, they're sometimes called "nitro-burning Funny Cars."

Fast Fact

The spoiler on a Funny Car works like an upside-down airplane wing. Instead of raising the car up into the air, it uses the wind's force to hold the car on the track.

Cruz Pedregon and a member of his racing team make a last-minute check before a race.

spoiler

SPEED UP, SLOW DOWN

Funny Cars have special tires. They're called "slicks" because they're smooth. This helps them stick to the track and speed forward. The force from the engine turns the huge back tires into ovals during a race. They look like cartoon tires!

Everyday cars go about 60 miles (97 km) per hour on the highway. Funny Cars can go 300 miles (480 km) per hour! When you're going that fast, ordinary brakes won't stop you. Funny Cars have two **parachutes** to help them stop.

Funny Car parachutes are called drag chutes.

Fast Fact Funny Car bodies need to be smooth and sleek to slide through the air. They're lightweight shells made of a matter called carbon fiber. Race teams paint wild patterns on them. Even the headlights and grills are painted on.

FUNNY CARS ON THE TRACK

Funny Car races are held on ¼-mile (400-m) tracks. Before a Funny Car is raced, the driver does a "burnout." Water is placed on part of the track. The driver **revs** the engine up to almost full power and drives through the water. This makes a lot of smoke and noise! Drivers do burnouts to heat up the tires and the track so the car gets the maximum **traction** at the start of the race. It's one of the fans' favorite parts of drag racing.

Fast Fact A racing series is a set of races for a certain type of vehicle. One series for Funny Cars is the National Hot Rod Association's (NHRA) Full Throttle Drag Racing Series.

Cruz Pedregon

Brothers Tony and Cruz Pedregon have each won two Funny Car Championships.

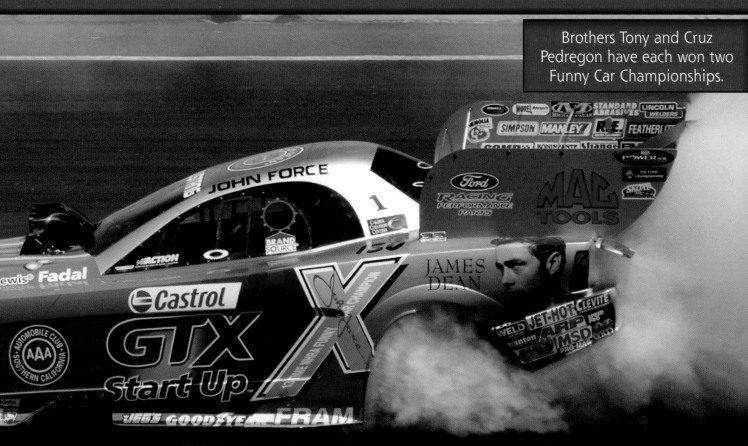

RACE TIME!

Once the drivers are ready to race, they must get into place on the starting line so that they both start from exactly the same position. This is called staging. It's done with the help of lights on the starting tree. Drivers are given the green light to start. They need good **reaction time**. A driver who doesn't leave the starting line the instant the light turns green will likely lose. A driver who leaves before the light turns green is said to "red light." That driver has lost the race before it's even started.

Fast Fact John Force, who is both a driver and a team owner, is a 14-time Funny Car Champion. No other drag racer has won as many championships.

The starting tree is a pole with the starting lights on it. It's sometimes called the Christmas tree.

starting tree

15

GOING FOR THE WIN

A Funny Car race takes just 4 seconds! There's a lot drivers need to do in a short amount of time on the way to the finish line. They need to know when to shift gears and speed up. They must be able to drive their Funny Cars down the track without blowing up the engine or going out of control and losing the race. Then they need to slow the car down from 300 miles (480 km) per hour to zero by "popping the chutes" so they don't go flying off the end of the track. Wow, what a ride!

Fast Fact Ashley Force Hood, the daughter of John Force, is the first woman to win a race in Funny Car. She also holds the top speed record for Funny Cars— 316.38 miles (509 km) per hour!

Ashley Force Hood

Racers Ronn Capps (left) and Jack Beckman speed down the track in Sonoma, California.

17

BETWEEN RACES

Once a race is over, racing teams head back to the **garage** to rebuild the car for the next race. This takes up to 75 minutes. Each team can have up to six **mechanics**. Each mechanic has a job to do. The engine must be taken apart and have new parts put into it. The drag chutes must be repacked and the car refueled. Any mistake in putting things back together could lead to problems. Computers are used to make sure everything works. Then it's back to the track to race and hopefully win a **trophy** as the top Funny Car racer!

Ron Capps poses with his trophy after winning the FRAM-Autolite NHRA Nationals in July 2010.

Fast Fact A Funny Car's back tires spin so quickly at the start of a race that the front end of the car can fly up in the air. A "wheelie bar" on the back of the car keeps the front end from going up. This helps the driver keep control of the car and get a lower ET.

19

FUNNY CAR SAFETY

In Funny Car races, crashes can happen. Exploding engines and losing control at high speeds are huge dangers. Nitromethane is a very explosive fuel, so drivers must wear fireproof suits. Each car has a driver-controlled system to stop fires. Every racetrack has safety workers who can reach an accident quickly. They put out fires and get drivers out of their cars. Modern racetracks are built to keep cars from hitting crowds. Most tracks have doctors and ways to get hurt drivers to hospitals quickly.

FUNNY CAR NUMBERS

Fastest ET	4.023 seconds, Ron Capps, 02/22/09
Fastest Speed	316.38 mph (509 kph), Ashley Force Hood, 03/27/10
Most Career Wins	128, John Force
First Funny Car Champion	Shirl Greer, 1974 (NHRA)
Most Championships	14, John Force

GLOSSARY

fuel: something that is burned to create power

garage: a building where race teams can fix a car

hot rod: a street car that has been made to go faster and look sportier

mechanic: a person who builds and fixes cars

parachute: a specially shaped piece of cloth that collects air to slow something down

reaction time: how long it takes to decide to do something

rev: to increase the speed of the engine

traction: the stickiness between two surfaces, such as a tire and the track

trophy: a prize awarded to the winner of a race

vehicle: an object that moves people from one place to another

FOR MORE INFORMATION

Books

Gigliotti, Jim. *Hottest Dragsters and Funny Cars*. Berkeley Heights, NJ: Enslow Publishers, 2008.

Kaelberer, Angie Peterson. *Funny Cars*. Mankato, MN: Capstone Press, 2006.

Von Finn, Denny. *Funny Cars*. Minneapolis, MN: Bellwether Media, 2009.

Web Sites

John Force Racing
www.johnforceracing.com
Read about Funny Car legend John Force and his teammates, including his daughter Ashley Force Hood.

The National Hot Rod Association (NHRA)
www.nhra.com
Keep up with Funny Car racing at the official NHRA Web site.

23

Publisher's note to educators and parents: Our editors have carefully reviewed these Web sites to ensure that they are suitable for students. Many Web sites change frequently, however, and we cannot guarantee that a site's future contents will continue to meet our high standards of quality and educational value. Be advised that students should be closely supervised whenever they access the Internet.

INDEX